IS-284: Using the Substantial Damage Estimator 2.0 Tool

By

Fema

1/2/2014

Course Summary: IS-284

Table of Contents:

Lesson 1:

Welcome

The SDE 2.0 tool was developed by FEMA to assist state & local officials in determining Substantial Damage for residential & non-residential structures in accordance with local floodplain management regulations meeting the requirements of the National Flood Insurance Program (NFIP).

The SDE 2.0 tool does NOT make Substantial Damage determinations; it is only a tool to assist in making these determinations.

The SDE 2.0 tool is based on the concept of using damage estimates for individual building elements to determine whether the structure as a whole is Substantially Damaged.

Course Overview

The goal of this course is to help you become proficient at using the SDE 2.0 tool. At the conclusion of this course, you will be able to:

1. Recognize SDE 2.0 tool terminology and definitions.
2. Navigate the SDE 2.0 tool main menu, the toolbars, Help button, and status bar.
3. Input property-record information and create an assessment for either residential or non-residential structures.
4. Indentify how to import, export, and review data.
5. Generate a Community Report, Structure & Percent Damage Report, Summary Report, Detailed Report, and geo-referenced files.
6. Produce a Summary Report and a Detailed Report for either residential or non-residential properties.
7. Apply SDE 2.0 database functions and assignment features for field inspector and supervisor coordination.

8. Identify resources to troubleshoot SDE 2.0 issues.
9. Locate best practices for use of the SDE 2.0 tool.

This course is divided into 7 lessons—each lesson has an instruction component and a review component.

The instruction component explains specific aspects of the SDE 2.0 tool, and most include an activity in which you practice what was covered in the instruction.

The review component of each lesson presents learning checks and hands-on activities using the SDE 2.0 tool to demonstrate that you mastered the lesson objectives.

The SDE 2.0 tool should already be installed on your computer. If you have not installed it, do so now. You can download the tool and the User Manual from the EMI website page (or the FEMA.gov website) where you found this course.

IMPORTANT: If you are installing SDE 2.0 on a computer which already has SDE 1.0 or SDE 1.1 installed, back up all SDE data using the export function and uninstall the previous version of SDE before installing SDE 2.0.

IMPORTANT: This course includes activities which require establishing a sample database. If you have a current database on your computer, export that database to a backup file. Do not import your original database back to the SDE 2.0 tool until after you have completed this course. Instructions for backing up a database are included in the User Manual.

Both the SDE 2.0 tool and User Manual 1 are required to complete this course.

Screen Features

- Click on the **Exit** button to close this window and access the menu listing all lessons of this course. You can select any of the lessons from this menu by simply clicking on the lesson title.
- Click on the **Glossary** button to look up key definitions and acronyms.
- Click on the **Help** button to review guidance and troubleshooting advice regarding navigating through the course.
- Track your progress by looking at the **Progress** bar at the top right of each screen. To see a numeric display, roll your mouse over the Progress bar area.
- Follow the bolded green instructions that appear on each screen in order to proceed to the next screen or complete a Knowledge Review or Activity.

- Click on the **Back** or the **Next** buttons at the top and bottom of screens to move backward or forward in the lesson. **Note**: If the **Next** button is **dimmed**, you must complete an activity before you can proceed in the lesson.

Navigating Using Your Keyboard

Below are instructions for navigating through the course using your keyboard.

- Use the Tab key to move forward through each screen's navigation buttons and hyperlinks, or Shift + Tab to move backwards. A box surrounds the button that is currently selected.

- Press Enter to select a navigation button or hyperlink.

- Use the arrow keys to select answers for multiple-choice review questions or self-assessment checklists. Then tab to the Submit button and press Enter to complete a Knowledge Review or Self-Assessment.

- **Warning:** Repeatedly pressing Tab beyond the number of selections on the screen may cause the keyboard to lock up. Use Ctrl + Tab to deselect an element or reset to the beginning of a screen's navigation links (most often needed for screens with animations or media).

- JAWS assistive technology users can press the Ctrl key to quiet the screen reader while the course audio plays.

Receiving Credit

You may take a test on the material covered in this course to demonstrate that you have learned the information.

To receive credit:

1. Complete all of the lessons. Each lesson will take between 10 and 30 minutes to complete. It is important to allow enough time to complete the course in its entirety.

REMEMBER... YOU MUST COMPLETE THE ENTIRE COURSE TO RECEIVE CREDIT. If you have to leave a lesson prior to doing the lesson review exercises, do not exit from the course or close your browser. If you exit from the course, you will need to start that lesson over again.

2. Pass the final exam. The last screen provides instructions on how to complete the final exam.

Lesson Summary

This completes this lesson. In this lesson you learned:

- What this course is about.
- How to complete this course.
- How to receive credit for this course.

Lesson 2:

Lesson Overview

This lesson introduces the general layout of the SDE 2.0 tool, the use of menus, the Help button, and the status bar.

After completing this lesson you will be able to:

- Select the appropriate database type when first using the SDE 2.0 tool.
- Recognize the different options available on the SDE 2.0 main menu.
- Identify the five menus located in the SDE 2.0 main toolbar.
- Identify the content within the nine sections of the main menu.
- Identify the SDE 2.0 Help button for additional information.
- Locate the status bar and recognize its use within the database.

Using SDE for the First Time

The first time the SDE 2.0 tool is run on a computer, the Database Information window will appear, helping you to select the database type and name the database.

There are three options in the drop-down menu for Select Database Type. They are:

- **Server**—Use this option if you are supervising Substantial Damage inspectors. It allows your SDE 2.0 database to be accessed by field inspectors to receive assignments.
- **Client**—Use this option if you are a field inspector. This creates a database for you to receive assignments from a supervisor using a Server database.
- **Stand Alone**—Use this option if you are neither a field inspector nor a supervisor. This option establishes a database for use by individuals without the need to send or receive assignments.

After selecting the type of database a name should be created for the database.

IMPORTANT: The selection of the database type can only be made when opening the SDE 2.0 tool for the first time.

To change this selection, export the current database to a file (see lesson 4), uninstall the SDE 2.0 tool from the computer, reinstall the SDE 2.0 tool to the computer, open the SDE 2.0 tool, select the new database type, and import the SDE database (see lesson 4).

This course was designed for use in the Stand Alone option; however you can take this course using the SDE 2.0 tool in any of these options.

SDE Main Menu

The SDE 2.0 main menu has nine sections:

1. Main Toolbar
2. View/Search All Records/Add Default Data
3. Create/Add a Report
4. Generate Geo File
5. Bulk Property Editor
6. Reports
7. Import/Export
8. Help
9. Status Bar

This lesson will review each of these sections.

SDE Main Toolbar

The main toolbar is available at the top of every screen within the SDE 2.0 tool, providing constant access to all menu-specific operations.

The main toolbar has five menus:

- File
- Tools
- Custom Fields
- Database Functions
- Help

Clicking on the **File** menu produces a drop-down menu with six options for creating or editing files within the SDE 2.0 tool:

- **New Residential Assessment** allows users to begin a residential assessment on either a new or existing property record.
- **New Non-Residential Assessment** allows you to begin a non-residential assessment on either a new or existing property record.
- **Recent Assessments** shows most recent assessment files used.
- **Save** saves the current assessment file.
- **Main Menu** returns you to the main menu.

- **Exit** exits the SDE 2.0 tool. Upon exiting you will be prompted to save any work you have done.

Clicking on the **Tools** menu produces a drop-down menu with seven tools for managing data including importing and exporting files, creating reports, and deleting data:

- **Longitude/Latitude Validation is (on/off)** allows, when turned "on", the SDE 2.0 tool to confirm that the longitude and latitude information entered into the database is appropriate for the inspection area.
- **Import** imports SDE 2.0 data from an external file, usually one that was exported from another computer using the SDE 2.0 tool.
- **Export** exports SDE 2.0 data from the SDE 2.0 tool to a file which can be imported by another computer using the SDE 2.0 tool.
- **Summary Report for Current Assessment** creates a Summary Report for the individual property record being viewed at the time within the SDE 2.0 tool.
- **Detailed Report for Current Assessment** creates a Detailed Report for the individual property record being viewed at the time within the SDE 2.0 tool.
- **Longitude Latitude Import/Export** imports or exports longitude latitude coordinates to and from the SDE 2.0 tool for use or verification with a GIS application.
- **Delete all SDE Data** erases all data in the SDE 2.0 tool.

These options will be discussed in detail later in this course.

Clicking on the **Custom Fields** menu opens a drop-down menu with a single option.

Add/Edit/Delete Custom Field allows you to create and display a maximum of three custom fields.

Custom fields can be established to capture any common relevant information not already captured in the SDE 2.0 tool—for example, whether or not a property owner was present during the inspection, or whether there are animals on the property. The data entered into the custom fields is not used in making a determination of Substantial Damage.

Clicking on the **Database Functions** provides you with three options for managing SDE 2.0 database files:

- **Update Database Name** modifies the name of the current database.
- **Enterprise Import** imports groups of property records to the current database.
- **Add Property** imports a single property record and/or assessment.

Under the **Help** menu is a link to a PDF copy of the SDE 2.0 tool's User Manual.

The SDE 2.0 User Manual covers the following topics:

- o SDE 2.0 tool background, development, and use in determining Substantial Damage determinations
- o Installation Instructions
- o Creating SDE Property Records and Assessments
- o Exporting SDE Data
- o Data Assignment Functions
- o SDE Reports
- o Acronyms and Abbreviations

The user manual provides details not found in this course. For example, it explains how internal calculations are made, provides background information on NFIP requirements, and explains where existing information may be found to import and populate fields within the SDE 2.0 tool.

View/Search All Records

The **View/Search All Records** section on the main menu provides access to existing property records and assessments in the SDE 2.0 database.

Clicking on **View/Search All Records** brings up this screen, listing all the property records in the database.

You can select the structure type, input a key word to search for, or select a specific field to narrow the search results.

Create/Add a Record

Click on **Create/Add a Record** to add new property records to an existing database.

Similar to the options available under the File menu, clicking on **Create/Add a Record** allows you to add data on a record in one of four ways:

- o Create New Property
- o Add a Residential Assessment
- o Add a Non-Residential Assessment

- o Enter Default Data

There is a difference between records and assessments within SDE 2.0:

- o *Records* involve <u>property data</u> prior to the addition of field collected data (address, owner, etc.)
- o *Assessments* include one or more records for a single structure that <u>contain field collected data</u> for a Substantial Damage determination.

Create a New Property—Clicking on this option opens a blank form for entering all the data required for a new residential or non-residential property record.

Add a Residential Assessment—Selecting this option creates a new residential assessment based on an existing property record. This is useful when assessing similar structures in a neighborhood.

Add a Non-Residential Assessment—Selecting this option creates a new non-residential assessment based on an existing non-residential property record. This is useful when assessing similar structures in an area.

Enter Default Data—This function opens a form for establishing standard data for up to 22 of the most commonly used data fields which can be applied to any new residential or non-residential property added to the database.

Generate Geo File

The **Generate Geo File** function creates a compressed Keyhole Markup Language (KML) file that can be used with geographic and spatial mapping programs.

Geo files may be used to run a quick check on the accuracy of the longitude and latitude information entered into the SDE 2.0 database. They can also be used to plot the longitude and latitude data on a GIS map.

KML files specify a set of features (place marks, images, polygons, 3D models, textual descriptions, etc.) for display in geospatial software.

When clicking on the **Generate Geo File** button, a message appears indicating that you are responsible for obtaining permission for use of freeware for anything other than personal use.

Clicking on the OK button generates the Geo File. When the process is complete, a message appears that provides the location where the Geo File was saved. For example:

Your data was exported to SDESpatialData_11_7_2012_2.kmz, which is located on your desktop.

Bulk Property Editor

The **Bulk Property Editor** opens a spreadsheet of all residential and non-residential records and assessments.

The **Bulk Property Editor** allows users to review and modify assessments within the database.

The spreadsheet lists all the database information for each property including the property's location, owner, and damage assessment information.

Reports

The **Reports** section of the home screen allows users to generate three types of reports:

- o   Community Report
- o   Structure & Percent Damage Report
- o   Summary Report

Community Report—this report displays all properties in a community for which the SDE 2.0 tool has data. The report includes the percent of damage the SDE 2.0 tool has calculated for each property, the basis for the value of the building, the basis for the cost of repair, the actual cash value of the structure and the type of structure.

Structure & Percent Damage Report—this report displays the owner's name, structure location, and percent of damage as calculated by the SDE 2.0 tool.

Summary Report—this report provides a full page report summarizing the information for each property in the database.

Import/Export

In the Import/Export section, you can do the following:

- o Import SDE records as individual property records and/or assessments by clicking on Import SDE 2.0 Data or in groups by clicking on Enterprise Import.
- o Create an Excel file containing all data within the database by clicking on Export to Excel.
- o Export SDE 2.0 property records and assessments in a format that can be loaded onto another computer running the SDE 2.0 tool by clicking on Export SDE Data.

Help

The two links in the Help section of the main menu direct users to an electronic copy of the SDE 2.0 User Manual, and to web references on the SDE 2.0 tool. The Help section is located in the lower right corner of the SDE 2.0 home screen.

- o The User Manual provides important information on what types of information need to be available to use the SDE 2.0 tool, where that information is available, and design aspects of the tool. The User Manual also provides troubleshooting tips, standard abbreviations, and other important information not included in this course.

The web references link opens the FEMA.gov website, which contains information on current disasters, preparedness, and all other aspects of FEMA operations

Status Bar

The status bar at the bottom of any screen provides a direct link back to the main menu and lists the most recently used functions of the SDE2.0 tool.

In this example, the status bar show that a user has viewed existing records, returned to the main menu, exported SDE data, and added a new property.

Lesson Summary

This completes the overview of the SDE 2.0 tool and its functions. In this lesson you learned how to:

- o   Select the appropriate database type when first using the SDE 2.0 tool and recognize the importance of this initial decision.
- o   Recognize the different options available on the SDE 2.0 main menu.
- o   Identify the five menus located in the SDE 2.0 main toolbar.
- o   Identify the content within the nine sections of the main menu.
- o   Identify the SDE 2.0 Help button for additional information.
- o   Locate the status bar and recognize its use within the database.

Lesson 3:

Lesson Overview

This lesson covers entering information into the database to establish a property record and create an assessment.

After completing this lesson you will be able to:

- Enter residential or non-residential property data into the SDE 2.0 tool database.
- Distinguish between property records and assessments.
- Identify the six tabs used to input data for residential and non-residential properties.
- Enter structure-assessment information into a residential and non-residential property record.

The SDE 2.0 Database

The SDE 2.0 tool stores a database on the hard drive of the computer. This database stores records of both residential and non-residential properties and any assessments that have been conducted on those properties.

Property *records* must exist before an *assessment* can be conducted. If a property record does not already exist on a property being assessed, you must create a property record for the structure by entering basic property data at the same time the assessment is being conducted.

Reminder: There is a difference between records and assessments within SDE 2.0:

- *Records* involve <u>property data</u> (address, owner, etc.) entered prior to the addition of field collected data.
- *Assessments* include field-collected data (damage to structure elements) for a single structure for use in a Substantial Damage determination.

Adding Information to the Database

SDE 2.0 includes several forms for adding information to the database.

The forms for residential properties and non-residential properties look the same, but some data-entry fields differ. Both forms have six tabs across the top:

- Address
- Structure/Damage/NFIP Info
- Cost

- Element Percentages
- Output Summary
- Files & Photos

All assessment data for the property are entered under these six tabs.

If a property record with a previous assessment already exists in the database, the results of that assessment will appear on a seventh tab.

In this course there should be no seventh tab for any property records because there were no previous property assessments on any of the existing property records.

Opening or Establishing an Assessment

If the property being assessed is already listed in the database, the assessment information can be added to the existing property record by selecting the **View/Search All Records** button on the SDE 2.0 main menu.

If the property being assessed needs to be added to the database, the property record and assessment information can be added by selecting the **Create/Add a Record** button on the SDE 2.0 main menu.

Selecting the **View/Search All Records** option from the SDE 2.0 tool main menu opens a window which lists all current property records and assessments in the database and a brief summary of each property.

From this list users can select the property they wish to assess and click on the **Edit** button on the right side of that property's summary. This action opens the data-entry form for the property.

Tips:
Click on the **Edit** button in the white band of the property listing (see red arrow in illustration). This will open the assessment.

Users can also view the most recent assessments by clicking on the **File** menu in the main toolbar at the top of the SDE 2.0 screen and selecting **Recent Assessments**.

Custom fields can be added, deleted, or edited in any assessment by clicking on the **Custom Fields** menu in the main toolbar at the top of the SDE 2.0 screen.

If the property being assessed is **not** in the database, the property and its assessment information can be added to the database by selecting the **Create/Add a Record** button on the SDE 2.0 main menu.

Selecting this option will open a small menu with four options: click on the links below for information on each option.

- Create New Property
- Add a Residential Assessment
- Add a Non-Residential Assessment
- Enter Default Data

Tips:
Users can also create a New Property record by clicking on the **Database Functions** menu in the main toolbar at the top of the SDE 2.0 screen and selecting **Add Property.**

Users can also add a new residential or non-residential assessment by clicking on the **File** menu in the main toolbar and selecting **New Residential Assessment** or **New Non-Residential Assessment.**

The **Create a New Property** option opens a window which allows you to create a new property record. Data on the property's owner, location, NFIP information and any custom fields are entered on this form.

Clicking the Save button at the bottom of this form creates the new record and automatically directs you to the data-entry form for the property.

If you attempt to save a property record without completing the form, color-coded icons appear to prompt you to complete the form:

- Green push-pin icons indicate empty or invalid fields that are suggested but not required for a valid assessment.
- Yellow push-pin icons appear next to empty or invalid fields that are required to complete a valid assessment but are not required before saving a property record. This information may be added later, if it is not available at the time the property record is being established.
- Red push-pin icons appear next to empty or invalid fields that are required before saving or completing a valid assessment.

Tips:
These push-pin icons will appear any time information is missing when you attempt to save the property record or assessment.

The **Add a Residential Assessment** option opens a window listing all the residential property records already in the database. This allows users to select a property that is similar to the property being assessed and to use that property's data as a starting point to create a new property record. This is particularly useful if homes in a neighborhood are all of similar construction and suffered similar damage.

You can select one of the existing property records in the database by checking the box to the left of the property listing and then clicking on the **Use Selected Property** button. This action will open the data-entry form.

If none of the existing property records closely matches the property being assessed, click on the **New Property** button and select **Create a New Property,** completing the form as discussed earlier.

The **Add a Non-Residential Assessment** option opens a window listing all the non-residential property records already in the database. This allows users to select a property that is similar to the property being assessed and to use that property's data as a starting point to create a new property record. This is particularly useful if non-residential structures in an area are of similar construction and suffered similar damage.

You may select one of the existing non-residential property records in the database by checking the box to the left of the property listing and then clicking on the **Use Selected Property** button. This action will open the data-entry form.

If none of the existing non-residential property records closely matches the property being assessed, click on the **New Property** button and select **Create a New Property**, completing the form as discussed earlier.

The **Enter Default Data** option opens a window which allows you to enter all data common to the property records being assessed in this database. Data include:

- City, state, county and ZIP information
- Date and type of damage
- Inspector's name and phone number
- NFIP data

Not all fields must be filled in. Only those fields most likely to be common to all property records being added to the database need to be completed. The information entered in this form can be changed in individual property records as necessary.

The **Create a New Property, Add a Residential Assessment,** and **Add a Non-Residential Assessment** options all lead to the same data-entry form.

Once that form is open, the data may be entered for the specific property being assessed.

Data is entered under the six tabs discussed earlier:

- Address
- Structure/Damage/NFIP Info
- Cost

- Element Percentages
- Output Summary
- Files & Photos

Address Tab

Under the address tab are five main sections.

- **Subdivision**
- **Building Address**
- **Community**
- **Mailing Address**
- **Custom Fields**

Some data on the Address tab must be provided to save the property record. The red, yellow, and green push pins are used to designate suggested and required fields.

Information on what data is entered in each field is covered in the SDE 2.0 User Manual.

Tip:
The **Carry Over Data From Previous Record** button (see blue arrow) allows you to use data from the previous property record when applicable. This pulls select information from the previous assessment performed. This can be useful if, for example, a series of structures on a single street are being assessed and there is information that would be the same for each structure.

It is, of course, very important that any property-specific information be edited for the current property to avoid duplication of records or future uncertainty about a record's contents.

Structure/Damage/NFIP Info Tab

Under the Structure/Damage/NFIP Info tab are six main sections.

- **Structure Attributes**
- **Structure Information**
- **Damage Information**
- **Inspector Information**
- **NFIP Information**
- **Community Information**

As with the Address tab, some data on the Structure/Damage/NFIP Info tab must be provided to save the property record. The same red, yellow, and green push pins are used to designate suggested and required fields.

Information on what data is entered in each field is covered in the SDE 2.0 user's manual.

The year of construction is entered in this section and must be provided in the full, four digit format.

Tip:
The **Carry Over Data From Previous Record** button (see blue arrow) allows you to use data from the previous record when applicable. This pulls select information from the previous assessment performed. This can be useful if, for example, a series of structures on a single street are being assessed and there is information that would be the same for each structure.

It is, of course, very important that any property-specific information be edited for the current property to avoid duplication of records or future uncertainty about a record's contents.

Cost Tab

Under the Cost tab are four main sections:

- **Square Footage**
- **Cost Adjustments**
- **Additional Adjustments**
- **Computed Actual Cash Value**

On this tab, enter a cost per square foot for the building, a geographic adjustment factor (if required), unit or lump-sum costs for adjustments when applicable, and select either the depreciation rating or enter an estimated depreciation percentage in order to determine the replacement value and Actual Cash Value (ACV) of the structure.

Tip:
Information on the formulas used to calculate data, as well as possible sources for the data can be found in the SDE 2.0 User Manual.

Information can also be found by clicking on the small question mark icons in each section of this tab.

In the Square Footage section, click on the **Calculate Square Footage** (fig.1) button to enter building dimensions, determine the area of the structure, and populate the Total Square Footage data field.

After clicking on the **Calculate Square Footage** button, a window appears that shows four building shapes (fig. 2). Select the shape that most closely matches the structure being assessed. When a building footprint shape is selected, another window is opened where you enter the estimated dimensions and number of stories of the building (fig. 3).

You also have the option of entering the total square footage manually if the building shape does not match any of the four options provided or if the total square footage is available from tax, GIS or other information.

Once the dimensions are entered click the **Save** button to calculate the total square footage and save the information.

Then click the **Save the Total Square Footage and Close Form** button to return to the **Cost** tab with the **Total Square Footage** field populated.

Element Percentages Tab

The **Element Percentages** tab uses twelve building-element categories to assist in determining an amount of **Total Estimated Damages for residential structures and seven elements for non-residential structures.**

The **Element %** column is pre-populated by the SDE 2.0 tool based on the information you have completed in the **Structure/Damage/NFIP** Info tab. This value is used to determine whether a structure is Substantially Damaged, which is then shown on the **Output Summary** tab.

Output Summary Tab

The **Output Summary** tab summarizes the computations for value of the building and cost of repairs/improvement, as well as the calculated damage percentage.

This tab also includes option boxes that allow you to select which damage estimate and building value to use in making the Substantial Damage determination. For information on these options, consult the User Manual.

If available, you may enter an estimated value for the **Percent of Existing Improvements and Repairs Pre-Disaster.** Guidance on estimated value and adjustment calculations can be found in the SDE 2.0 User Manual.

Tip:
When all the information has been entered for a structure you can click on Print Summary Report or Print Detailed Report, using the buttons at the bottom of the tab, to view and print these documents.

Files & Photos Tab

The **Files & Photos** tab is used to upload and store photographs and files (e.g., maps, drawings, permits) associated with the subject structure which provide backup information for the estimate.

Following the onscreen instructions, select the button labeled **Select Photo/File** and choose the file to be added.

Once one or more files have been added, users may select the **Set as Default** option under the file to be displayed in the Summary Report and Community Report for that assessment.

Tip:
Large file sizes can slow down the computer's ability to run the SDE 2.0 tool. For this reason, it is recommended that files uploaded do not exceed a maximum size of 3 MB per file.

Review Activity

This lesson includes an activity which you will complete using the SDE 2.0 tool installed on your computer.

The activity includes instructions and all data necessary to practice what you learned in this lesson.

After downloading and printing the activity, click on the Next button to view the summary for this lesson. Then, exit this course while you conduct the activity using the SDE 2.0 tool.

Once you have completed the activity return to this course and advance to the review section for this lesson. You will be asked several questions based on the activity.

Lesson Summary

This concludes the lesson on populating a database. In this lesson you learned how to:

- Enter residential and non-residential property-record data into the SDE 2.0 tool.
- Distinguish between property records and assessments.
- Identify the six tabs used to input data for residential and non-residential assessments.
- Enter structure-assessment information into a residential and non-residential property records.

Lesson 4:

Lesson Overview

This lesson covers how data is imported and exported to and from the SDE 2.0 tool and how data can be reviewed within the SDE 2.0 tool.

After completing this lesson you will be able to:

- Import SDE 2.0 data exported from another computer running the SDE 2.0 tool.
- Identify how to conduct a data Enterprise Import.
- Export SDE 2.0 assessment files to a Microsoft Excel file.
- Identify how to export SDE 2.0 files in a format that can be imported to another computer running the SDE 2.0 tool.
- Review an SDE database for accuracy.

Importing/Exporting Data

The Import/Export section of the SDE 2.0 tool has the following options:

- Import SDE Data
- Enterprise Import
- Export Files to Excel
- Export SDE Data

The next four screens in this lesson will detail the steps for each of these options

Tips:

If users have access to pre-existing databases of property data, these databases can often be easily adapted for import into the SDE 2.0 tool. Check with your Assessor, GIS, E911 or other departments for existing property data.

Import SDE Data

To import data, click on the **Import SDE Data** link on the SDE main menu.

This will bring up a screen on which you must click on the **Select Directory** button.

This will open a window named **Browse for Folder.** You can then select the location where the SDE 2.0 files to be imported are located.

Data that have been exported from another computer using the SDE 2.0 tool will be located in a folder titled **SDE Assessments.**

Find the folder, highlight it, and click the **OK** button.

The SDE Data files will be listed in the table shown on the screen. Select the files to be imported by checking the box next to each desired property or assessment.

Individual files can be selected or the entire grouping can be selected by clicking on the **Check All** button.

Import the files by clicking the **Import** button

Once complete, you will see a window indicating that the files have been successfully imported.

Click the OK button to complete this task.

Enterprise Import

The **Enterprise Import** function is used to import multiple properties at one time. This can be a very useful function for large numbers of assessments, and any number of the available fields may be selected for importing.

Begin the process by clicking on the **Enterprise Import** button on the main menu.

After selecting the **Get File** button, you will be prompted to browse and select the file to be imported.

On-screen prompts will then ask questions specific to the type of file selected for import.

In this example, records are being importing from an Excel spreadsheet.

Click the **Format Excel** button.

When asked if this Excel sheet contains column headers, answer **yes** if appropriate. This will depend upon the format of the source data.

Once the data has loaded, click on the **Import Using This Format** button.

You will see a data-entry field for each type of data used in the SDE 2.0 tool.

In the **Select a Field** section, simply select the Excel spreadsheet column heading that contains the data needed for the SDE field.

For example, in the **Owner's First Name** field, select the field **Structure Owner's First Name.**

In the **Owner's Last Name** field, select the column heading **Structure Owner's Last Name.**

Do this for each field.

Finally, click the **Import Data** button and wait for confirmation that the data has been imported.

Click the OK button to complete this task.

Export Files to Excel

The **Export to Files Excel** function allows you to export all of the data located in the tool to an Excel file.

Start by selecting the **Export Files to Excel** button on the SDE 2.0 tool main menu.

A screen will appear allowing you to select the data to be exported to the Excel file.

Under **Structure Type** select Residential, Non-Residential, or Both.

You may also specify inspection dates or a range of percent damaged if desired.

Under the **Select Field** area, you may select any or all of the fields in the SDE 2.0 database. **View All Records** is used to export all the records in the SDE 2.0 database.

Clicking on the **Filter Results** button will cause all the records that match the chosen criteria to be displayed.

Clicking on the **Export Data** button will cause all the displayed records to be exported to an Excel Spreadsheet.

When the export is complete, the SDE 2.0 tool displays a message showing where the file is located.

Click **OK** to complete this process.

Export SDE Data

The Export SDE Data function allows you to export all the data located in the tool to an SDE file.

Like the Export to Excel function, once Export SDE data has been selected from the main menu, the next screen displayed will allow you to select the data to be exported to the SDE data file.

You may choose to export all data, or may filter the data to be exported by residential or non-residential structures, by inspection dates, by damage assessment, or other specific fields.

By selecting the Filter Results button, you will be presented with a detailed list of the property records which can be exported.

You can then select which property records to export by checking each one individually or by clicking on the Check All button to select all the property records listed

Export the files by clicking the Export button.

Click OK to save the file.

When the export is complete, the SDE tool displays a message showing where the file is located.

Click OK to complete the process.

Reviewing Databases

Property records and assessments can be reviewed for accuracy in any of the exported file formats.

For example, all SDE 2.0 data can be exported to an Excel spreadsheet where the data can be reviewed for accuracy.

- Note that this is a one way transfer of data. Data revisions made in the Excel file cannot be imported back into the SDE 2.0 tool.

However the SDE 2.0 tool has a special feature specifically for record review. This is the **Bulk Property Editor.**

By clicking on the Bulk Property Editor button on the main menu, users can view all property records right in the SDE 2.0 tool.

Users can sort and filter these property records in exactly the same manner as when exporting or importing files. Changes to files can be made within the Bulk Property Editor screen.

Review Activity

This lesson includes an activity which you will complete using the SDE 2.0 tool installed on your computer.

The activity includes instructions and all data necessary to practice what you learned in this lesson.

After downloading and printing the activity, click on the Next button to view the summary for this lesson. Then, exit this course while you conduct the activity using the SDE 2.0 tool.

Once you have completed the activity, return to this course and advance to the review section for this lesson. There you will be asked several questions based on the activity.

Lesson Summary

This lesson covered how data is imported and exported to and from the SDE 2.0 tool and how data can be reviewed within the SDE 2.0 files.

In this lesson you learned how to:

- Import SDE 2.0 data exported from another computer running the SDE 2.0 tool.
- Identify how to conduct a data Enterprise Import.
- Export SDE 2.0 assessment files to a Microsoft Excel file.
- Identify how to export SDE 2.0 files in a format that can be imported to another computer running the SDE 2.0 tool.
- Review an SDE database for accuracy.

Lesson 5:

Lesson Overview

This lesson covers the three primary types of reports the SDE 2.0 tool can generate, and the various options available in each report type.

After completing this lesson you will be able to:

- Identify how to properly create a Community Report for a given community.
- Identify how to properly create Structure and Percent Damage Reports from the main menu.
- Identify ways to create a Summary Report and a Detailed Report.
- Create a Summary Report and a Detailed Report.

Creating Reports from the Main Menu

The **Reports** section of the SDE 2.0 tool main menu shows the following options for creating reports:

- Community Report
- Structure and Percent Damage Report
- Summary Report

When the reports are opened within the tool, users have the option to either view or print the reports for all assessments in the inventory or for specific assessments using one or more of the available report filter criteria.

The next three screens in this lesson will detail the steps for each of these options.

Tip:
Reports can also be created by clicking on the **Tools** menu on the main toolbar and selecting the type of report you want to create.

Community Report

A Community Report provides summary information on an entire community.

The report shows the following information:

- Address (shown just above the data below)
- Owner's Name

- Percent Damage of the Structure
- Basis for the Value of the Building
- Basis for the Cost of Repairs
- Actual Cash Value of the Home
- Type of Structure
- Photo of the structure (if included in the assessment and listed as the default image).

This report can be generated from the main menu by clicking the Community Report icon in the Reports section.

After clicking on Community Report you are given the option to choose which type of structure to include in the report.

In the Structure Type drop down menu, select Residential, Non-residential, or Both.

If you want to generate a report including only assessments made on a particular date or that resulted in a specific range of percent damage, those parameters can be indicated in the Filter By section.

In the Select Field drop down menu, users can specify which fields within the SDE 2.0 database they want included in the report.

When these options are complete, click on the Get Reports button to generate the report.

The report can be viewed within the SDE 2.0 tool, or printed by clicking on the Print button.

If the report is more than one page long, the pages of the report can be accessed by clicking the Next button above the report content.

Structure and Percent Damage Report

A Structure and Percent Damage Report provides structure and damage information on properties in a community.

The report shows the following information:

- Address
- Owner's Name
- City and State
- County

- Percent Damage
- Photo of the structure (if included in the assessment and listed as the default image).

This report can be generated from the main menu by clicking the Structure and Percent Damage Report icon in the Reports section.

After clicking on Structure and Percent Damage you are given the option to choose which type of structure to include in the report.

In the Structure Type drop down menu, select Residential, Non-residential, or Both.

If you want to generate a report including only assessments made on a particular date or that resulted in a specific range of percent damage, those parameters can be indicated in the Filter By section.

In the Select Field drop down menu, users can specify which fields within the SDE 2.0 database they want included in the report.

When these options are complete, click on the Get Reports button to generate the report.

The report can be viewed within the SDE 2.0 tool, or printed by clicking on the Print button.

If the report is more than one page long, the pages of the report can be accessed by clicking the Next button above the report content.

Summary Report

A Summary Report provides a one-page summary of each structure within the community database.

This report can be generated from the main menu by clicking the Summary Report icon in the Reports section.

After clicking on Summary Report the user is given the option to choose which type of structure to include in the report.

In the Structure Type drop down menu, select Residential, or Non-residential. There is no option for including both residential and non-residential properties in this report.

If you want to generate a report including only assessments made on a particular date or that resulted in a specific range of percent damage, those parameters can be indicated in the Filter By section.

In the Select Field drop down menu, users can specify which fields within the SDE 2.0 database they want included in the report.

When these options are complete, click on the Get Reports button to generate the report.

The report for each structure appears on a different page within the SDE 2.0 tool. The pages can be accessed by clicking on the Next button above the Summary Report content.

The report can be viewed within the SDE 2.0 tool, or printed by clicking on the Print button.

Creating Reports from the Output Summary Tab

Individual structure Summary Reports are also available through the Output Summary tab, which is one of the six tabs used to input property record and assessment data for a structure (See Lesson 3).

Under the Output Summary tab, users can create the same one-page Summary Report for the property for which they are inputting data.

In addition to this one page Summary Report, a five page Detailed Report is also available.

Generating a Summary Report

To generate a Summary Report for a specific property, start at the SDE 2.0 main menu.

Click on the View/Search Records button.

Select the property for the report and click on the Edit icon.

When the data form appears on the screen, select the Output Summary tab.

Scroll to the bottom of the page and click on the Print Summary Report for This Structure button.

A one page Summary Report for the structure will appear on the screen.

To print this report, click on the Print icon above the report.

Generating a Detailed Report

To generate a Detailed Report for a specific property, start at the SDE 2.0 main menu.

Click on the View/Search Records button.

Select the property for the report and click on the Edit icon.

When the data form appears on the screen, select the Output Summary tab.

Scroll to the bottom of the page and click on the Print Detailed Report For This Structure button.

A five- page Detailed Report for the structure will appear on the screen.

To view each page of the report, click on the Next button above the report content.

To print this report, click on the Print icon above the report.

Review Activity

This lesson includes an activity which you will complete using the SDE 2.0 tool installed on your computer.

The activity includes instructions and all data necessary to practice what you learned in this lesson.

After downloading and printing the activity, click on the Next button to view the summary for this lesson. Then, exit this course while you conduct the activity using the SDE 2.0 tool.

Once you have completed the activity, return to this course and advance to the review section for this lesson. There you will be asked several questions based on the activity.

Lesson Summary

This lesson covered the three primary types of reports the SDE 2.0 tool can generate, and the various options available in each report type.

In this lesson you learned how to:

- Identify how to properly create a Community Report for a given community.
- Identify how to properly create Structure and Percent Damage Reports from the main menu.
- Identify ways to create a Summary Report and a Detailed Report.
- Create a Summary Report and a Detailed Report.

Lesson 6:

Lesson Overview

This lesson covers setting up the SDE 2.0 tool as a server, client, or stand alone tool depending on who is using the tool and how it will be used.

After completing this lesson you be able to:

- Recognize when to use the Server option as a database type.
- Recognize when to use the Client option as a database type.
- Recognize when to use the Stand Alone option as a database type.

Server, Client, and Stand Alone Options

The first time the tool is run after installation, you have the option of selecting the database type as a **Server, Client**, or **Stand Alone**.

For an explanation of each of these options, click on the links below:

- Server
- Client
- Stand Alone

Server Option:

This option is designed for those people responsible for supervising field inspectors. This gives supervisors the ability to send assignments to field inspectors.

Client Option:

This option is designed for field inspectors.
This gives field inspectors the ability to receive assignments from supervisors.

Stand Alone Option:

This option is designed for users of SDE 2.0 who are neither field inspectors nor their supervisors.
This group would include people who work for local governments, quality control personnel, and data analysts.

Once the SDE 2.0 tool has been set up as a server, client, or stand alone tool, it cannot be changed without uninstalling and reinstalling the SDE 2.0 tool.

Before uninstalling the SDE 2.0 tool, back up all files by using the Export SDE 2.0 function on the main menu.

Complete instructions on how to use the SDE 2.0 tool as either a server or a client are included in the User Manual beginning on page 3-1.

Because these functions are specific to a limited audience, they are not covered in this course.

Lesson Summary

This lesson covered setting up the SDE 2.0 tool as a server, client, or stand alone tool depending on who is using the tool and how it will be used.

In this lesson you learned how to:

- Recognize when to use the Server option as a database type.
- Recognize when to use the Client option as a database type.
- Recognize when to use the Stand Alone option as a database type.

Lesson 7:

Lesson Overview

This lesson covers troubleshooting, best practices and frequently asked questions about the SDE 2.0 tool

After completing this lesson you will be able to:

- Locate the resources for resolving technical issues with the SDE 2.0 tool.
- Recognize where to find best practices to help address problems which may be experienced when using the SDE 2.0 tool.

Trouble Shooting

Technical assistance with the SDE tool is available through the Mitigation Division Director of the FEMA regional office for your state.

Best Practices

FEMA has identified a series of best practices for using the SDE 2.0 tool. These best practices cover Planning Data Collection, Field Work, and Data Management.

Lesson Summary

This completes the final lesson in this course.

In this lesson you learned how to:

- Locate the resources for resolving technical issues with the SDE 2.0 tool.
- Recognize where to find best practices to help address problems which may be experienced when using the SDE 2.0 tool.

www.ingramcontent.com/pod-product-compliance
Lightning Source LLC
Chambersburg PA
CBHW081324250726

48662CB00008B/2739